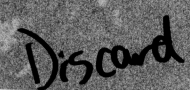

FREDERICK DOUGLASS

The Lion Who Wrote History

by

Walter Dean Myers

illustrated by

Floyd Cooper

Quill Tree Books
An Imprint of HarperCollinsPublishers

This is the story of how one man's careful decisions and many accomplishments not only made his own life better but in many ways changed the history of America.

Frederick Augustus Washington Bailey was born a slave in Talbot County, Maryland, in 1818. His grandmother, Betsey Bailey, was also a slave, and she took care of young Frederick.

When he was about nine, he was sent to live with slave owner Hugh Auld and his family. He was given chores to do around the house and helped care for the family's children.

Soon after he arrived, Frederick saw Sophia Auld, the mistress of the house, teaching her children to read. He wanted to learn too. Seeing how eager he was, Mrs. Auld started giving him lessons along with her own children.

But when Hugh Auld found out that his wife was teaching Frederick to read, he objected. "Teaching a slave to read will make him unfit to be a slave," Mr. Auld said.

Sophia was not happy, but she understood what her husband meant: the ability to read would expose slaves to ideas and information that would make them unhappy being "owned" by someone else. Frederick also understood what Mr. Auld was saying. He thought hard about how the slave owner linked reading with slavery.

Frederick listened carefully to the Auld children. They spoke clearly and directly, and he knew that it was because they had also read the words they used. He felt that reading could make a difference in how a person lived.

As he grew up in the Auld household, Frederick was becoming aware of what it meant to be a slave. Slaves were forced to work for their owners. As punishment, they could be beaten, and they could be sold away from their families.

Frederick watched as the Auld children received an education. He listened as they excitedly shared their ideas and dreams with friends. Theirs sounded like a good life, and he wanted the same chance to build a good life for himself.

If learning to read would make him unfit to be a slave, then that's what Frederick would do: He made the courageous decision to learn to read. It would be very difficult, because slaves were not allowed to go to school or have books to practice reading. When he could, he borrowed books from the young white friends he sometimes played with. He picked up old newspapers and flyers he found in the streets. Anything that contained precious words was important to Frederick.

By the time he was sixteen, Frederick was tall, well built, and very unhappy with his life. He was also a reader and a young man who used words well. Sometimes he used them unwisely. After he argued with his master, he was sent to Edward Covey, a man known for making slaves less likely to stand up for themselves. He would bully the black men and women and beat them until they gave up the struggle to be more than slaves. Frederick was beaten viciously every week when he was with Covey. But one day, the slave breaker tried to beat him again, and he decided to fight back, even if it meant his death. The two men struggled furiously for more than half an hour. In the end it was Covey who gave up against the now-strong Frederick. Covey never tried to beat Frederick again.

Frederick was hired out to the shipyards. He became a caulker, a hard job that took strong hands and careful attention as he put tar and heavy cord between the boards of ships to make them waterproof. Most of the money he earned went to his master. But, for the first time, Frederick was meeting free black men. Many of them sailed the very ships he was repairing.

Free black sailors had always been a problem for slaveholders. They had papers proving they were free and were able to walk around most ports as they chose. The tales of their adventures spread among the enslaved blacks. Frederick listened to them carefully and imagined himself being as free as they were.

When he was nineteen, Frederick fell in love with a free black woman, Anna Murray. But he was a slave and could not be with her as he chose. The lure of freedom became almost unbearable, but to try to escape was a risky business. Slaveholders did not want to lose their precious "property." When slaves who tried to escape were caught, they were often punished severely.

Frederick knew he had to take the chance!

In September 1838, Frederick made his move. Using the seaman's papers of a free black sailor and dressing like the sailors he saw on his job, he boarded a train headed north.

"I suppose you have your free papers?" the conductor asked him.

"No, sir, I never carry my free papers to sea with me," Frederick said. "Here are my seaman's papers."

The conductor looked at the papers. "You don't sound as if you're from around here," he said.

"I haven't been around here much," Frederick said, holding his breath.

The conductor gave Frederick a hard look and then accepted his fare.
"I don't think you'd like it very much in these parts," he said.

After the train ride Frederick took a ferry across the Susquehanna River into Pennsylvania, and then he took another train to New York City. Frederick arrived at the home of an abolitionist whose name he had been given.

"Sir, I can use some help." Frederick was almost trembling as he spoke to the man who answered the door.

"Come in, come in," the man said. "You've come to the right place."

Frederick entered the house and breathed a sigh of relief. He had escaped.

Anna Murray soon joined him in
New York, where they were married. After
a short while they made their way to New Bedford,
Massachusetts. In 1838, New Bedford was a city with a small
but strong black population. It was nicknamed "the whaling city"
because there were always whaleboats in its harbor, and Frederick was sure that
he could find a job. Frederick loaded and unloaded ships, sawed wood, and hauled
coal—anything to make a living.

Afraid that slave catchers might be looking for him, Frederick Augustus Washington
Bailey decided to rename himself. He was now Frederick Douglass.

He was very impressed by the people he met in New Bedford. All of them were hardworking sailors or dockworkers, and many of them were abolitionists who spoke passionately about the rights of all people. In turn, the abolitionists were impressed by Douglass. Here was a man who could actually tell people what it was like to be a slave. He had been forced to work for his white master. He had been beaten. His sisters had been sold away from the family. Not only could he tell of his experiences, but he could speak with an eloquence that stirred the souls of his audience.

Douglass was often asked by the abolitionist society to speak at their meetings. Some people who heard him could hardly believe that he had ever been a slave. They wondered if all the black people working in the fields or on Southern plantations had the potential of this tall and handsome young man.

Douglass was also asked to write the story of his life. In 1845, when he was only twenty-seven years old, his autobiography, *Narrative of the Life of Frederick Douglass, an American Slave*, was published.

Frederick Douglass understood how his speaking helped to bring

people into the fight against the evils of slavery and for the equality of all human beings. In 1848, at a convention for women's rights held in Seneca Falls, New York, his powerful speech convinced the male delegates to pass an important amendment demanding that women be allowed to vote.

"I have never yet been able to find one consideration, one argument, or suggestion in favor of man's right to participate in civil government which did not equally apply to the right of woman," Douglass said.

Frederick Douglass spent years speaking for the rights of black people and women. During those years the differences between the agricultural South, with its cotton, rice, and other crops, and the more industrial North, with its large cities and factories, grew more distinct.

In 1859, Frederick Douglass was contacted by John Brown, a militant white abolitionist. John Brown was passionate about freedom. He had heard the language of other abolitionists and saw that, for the most part, slaveholders paid no attention to them. "These men are all talk," he said. "What we need is action—action!"

In Chambersburg, Pennsylvania, Brown shared his plan with Frederick Douglass. It was risky, but to John Brown it was a lot more plausible than the do-nothing plans of other abolitionists. If Frederick Douglass would be part of his plan, there would be a great chance of its working.

"Here is a chance to put the question to everyone that has ever held a slave, and to this country!" Brown said to Douglass when they met.

Douglass thought hard and carefully. Brown's plan was to capture the federal arsenal at Harpers Ferry, then take the weapons into the hills.

"To me you are entering a perfect steel trap," Frederick said. "And one from which you will not get out of alive."

Shortly after their meeting, John Brown led the raid on the arsenal at Harpers Ferry on October 16, 1859. The raiders succeeded in capturing part of the grounds at Harpers Ferry and taking a number of hostages, but in the end the raid failed, as Douglass thought it would.

The conflict between the Northern and Southern states came to a head in December 1860, when the Southern states began to secede from the Union. They decided to form their own country, the Confederate States of America. President Abraham Lincoln ordered American forces, called the Union Army, to put down what he considered simple rebellion and treason. The battles between the North and South went on for three long and bloody years without either side gaining a decisive advantage. The Union Army was made up of white soldiers, with some blacks used as laborers. Douglass urged the Union to enlist black soldiers. In 1863, shortly after the battle of Gettysburg, he met with President Lincoln and urged the president to enlist black soldiers as equals in the Union Army.

"I saw in this war the end of slavery," Douglass declared. "I urged every man of color who could, to enlist; to get an eagle on his button, a musket on his shoulder, and the star-spangled banner over his head.

"The iron gate of our prison stands half open. One gallant rush from the North will fling it wide open, while four millions of our brothers and sisters shall march out into liberty!"

One hundred eighty thousand black soldiers, many of whom had been born in slavery, joined the Union Army. They helped to defeat the Confederacy in 1865.

In 1865 the Thirteenth Amendment to the United States Constitution was enacted to legally end slavery in the United States.

The careful and wise decisions made by Frederick Douglass—to learn to read, to escape from slavery, to speak out for justice for all Americans, and to aid the Union Army—had helped to write American history.

Frederick Douglass, born a slave, continued to work and speak for the rights of all Americans. He served the United States government in Washington as well as in Haiti as consul-general. His voice, born in the soft tones of the slave population, truly became a lion's roar.

Timeline of Frederick Douglass's Life

1818 Frederick Augustus Washington Bailey is born in Talbot County, Maryland.

1827 Frederick begins learning to read in the Auld household.

1834 Frederick is "rented out" to Edward Covey, who beats him constantly.

1837 Frederick meets Anna Murray, a free black woman who washes clothes.

1838 Using a sailor's papers, he escapes to the North.

1840 He lectures with the New Bedford Anti-Slavery Society.

1845 He publishes *Narrative of the Life of Frederick Douglass, an American Slave.*

1845 He travels to Ireland.

1846 British sympathizers raise money to buy Douglass's freedom from Hugh Auld. Many antislavery people objected to this, saying that it was participation in the slave trade. Douglass realized, however, that as long as he was legally the "property" of Auld, he could be kidnapped and sent back to his master.

1848 Frederick attends the Seneca Falls Convention for women's rights.

1850 He publishes several newspapers, including the *North Star* and *Douglass' Monthly.*

1859 He meets with John Brown and discusses a possible raid on Harpers Ferry.

1863 The Emancipation Proclamation is issued.

1863 He recruits soldiers for the 54th and other regiments. His son Lewis fights with the 54th Regiment.

1865 The Thirteenth Amendment is ratified, prohibiting slavery.

1865–1895 Frederick holds various government posts, including U.S. minister-resident and consul-general to Haiti.

1895 Frederick Douglass dies at 77.

Bibliography

Douglass, Frederick. *The Life and Times of Frederick Douglass.* Cleveland: Hamilton, Rewell & Company, 1883.

———. *My Bondage and My Freedom.* New York: Miller, Orton & Mulligan, 1855.

———. *A Narrative of the Life of Frederick Douglass, an American Slave, Written by Himself.* Boston: Anti-Slavery Office, 1845.

Douglass' Monthly, 1858–1863.

Document signed by Hugh Auld officially freeing Frederick Douglass

To all whom it may concern: Be it known that I, Hugh Auld of the City of Baltimore, in Baltimore County in the State of Maryland, for divers good causes and considerations me thereunto moving, have released from slavery, liberated, manumitted, and set free, and by these presents do hereby release from slavery, liberate, manumit, and set free, MY NEGRO MAN named FREDERICK BAILEY, otherwise called DOUGLASS, being of the age of twenty-eight years or thereabouts, and able to work and gain a sufficient livelihood and maintenance; and him, the said negro man named FREDERICK DOUGLASS, I do declare to be henceforth free, manumitted, and discharged from all manner of servitude to me, my executors and administrators forever.

In witness whereof, I, the said Hugh Auld, have hereunto set my hand and seal the fifth of December, in the year one thousand eight hundred and forty-six.

Hugh Auld

For those who are, and aspire to be, self-made.
—F.C.

Quill Tree Books is an imprint of HarperCollins Publishers.
Frederick Douglass: The Lion Who Wrote History
Text copyright © 2017 by Walter Dean Myers and the Estate of Walter Myers
Illustrations copyright © 2017 by Floyd Cooper
All rights reserved. Manufactured in Italy.
No part of this book may be used or reproduced in any manner whatsoever without written permission except in the case of brief quotations embodied in critical articles and reviews. For information address HarperCollins Children's Books, a division of HarperCollins Publishers, 195 Broadway, New York, NY 10007.
www.harpercollinschildrens.com

Library of Congress Cataloging-in-Publication Data
Myers, Walter Dean, 1937–2014.
 Frederick Douglass : the lion who wrote history / by Walter Dean Myers ; illustrated by Floyd Cooper. — First Edition.
  pages cm
 Audience: Grades K to 3.
 ISBN 978-0-06-027709-3 (hardcover)—ISBN 978-0-06-303792-2 (paperback)
 1. Douglass, Frederick, 1818–1895—Juvenile literature. 2. Slaves—United States—Biography—Juvenile literature.
3. Abolitionists—United States—Biography—Juvenile literature. 4. African American abolitionists—Biography—Juvenile
literature. 5. Antislavery movements—United States—History—Juvenile literature. 6. African Americans—History—19th
century—Juvenile literature. I. Cooper, Floyd, illustration. II. Title.
E449.D75M96 2016   2014041206
973.8092—dc23   CIP
[B]   AC

The artist used erasers & oils on board to create the illustrations for this book.
Typography by Rachel Zegar
21 22 23 24 25 RTLO 13 12 11 10 9 8 7 6 5 4
❖
First Edition

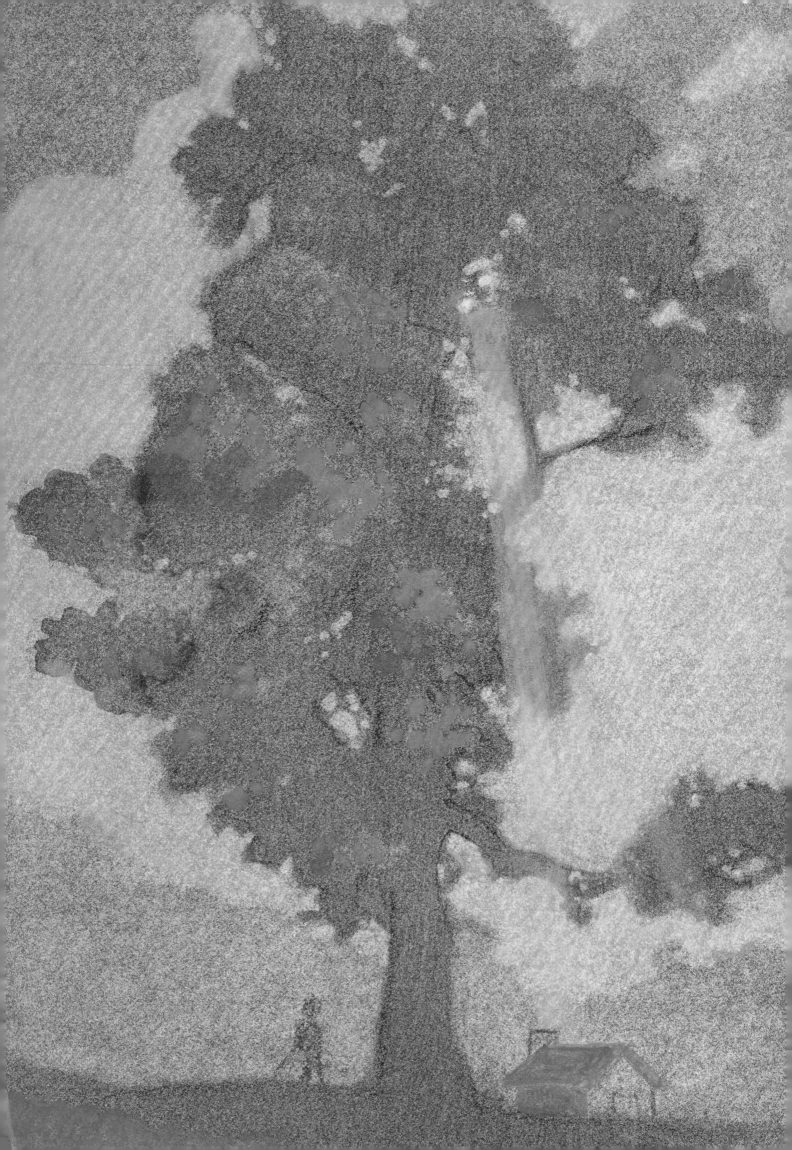